Buy/Sell/Trade:

What you need to know!

Information by Bryan Desjardins

Written by Roxanne Petersik

Feel free to also visit/like/share and follow us:

Like our page on Facebook at www.facebook.com/ roxannepetersikauthor

Send us a tweet and follow us on Twitter at @RoxannePetersik or twitter.com/RoxannePetersik

Follow us on Google+ at google.com/+RoxannePetersikAuthor

Subscribe to us on YouTube at youtube.com/c/ RoxannePetersikAuthor

Send us an email to join our list for news, upcoming books and release dates at roxannepetersik@gmail.com

Table of Contents

Preface

Have you ever heard of someone getting a great deal on an item like a car, and thought to yourself " I wish I could get great deals like that, but I don't know how to."

After reading this book you can put all my tips and tricks into action and start getting yourself great deals too.

We designed this book to be a short read basics book that will give you the information you need, but that will allow you to put the information into action as soon as possible.

Honestly, we could probably write a book for each chapter we have provided information on, but that would take way too much time to read and would be harder to remember to put all the information into real life action.

I have been in the buying, repairing and selling business for about 10 years, and have nearly perfected the art of not only negotiation, but reading people in order to know how best to make a deal for myself.

I have so many ways of working with people to get a great deal that I almost always come out on top (I will also explain later in this book how you can end up blowing a deal). But all buyers and sellers have different personalities, and not all of my tactics will work for each situation.

So after being asked numerous times by people how I do what I do, I have decided to write a book on the basics of what I do. But before we get into it, I believe it helps to know a bit about where it all started for me, to get an idea on how I developed my skills.

About 10 years ago I had nothing but some mechanical skills for working on cars and a love of riding dirt bikes, quads and snowmobiles. I also had a Honda 350 cc motorcycle that I used to ride around as my vehicle before I bought another car.

I decided one day that I wanted to go ATVing again, but we had only a little bit of money to buy something to ride. So my girlfriend and I went to a motorsport recyclers and bought a dirt bike and trike in need of repairs for $500. They needed quite a bit of work to get going in order to get out riding, but we put both of our skill sets and knowledge together, and got them looking and running great.

We rode them for a while, then when we were ready and able to upgrade to some better machines we sold them, and made a pretty good profit from what we had originally spent. At that point I realized that maybe we could buy machines that were in need of repair for cheap, fix them, and then sell them for a bit more money than we had originally spent and make a profit.

It was a light bulb moment that changed my life, and brought me to where I am today. And now after nearly 10 years of searching and negotiating for good deals on everything in my life, and teaching myself everything along the way, including how to fix everything I bought, I have decided to teach others about the art of buying and selling items to improve their lives.

Everyone wants a good price on items they need or want in their life, and in this book I will explain the basics of my knowledge on how to get great deals.

But be warned, it can become a very addicting process, and you may enjoy getting good deals so much that you may find yourself using these skills in all aspects of buying and/or selling in your life.

In this book we have laid out the process of buying and selling from start to finish, and in each chapter we go over each aspect for first a buyer (as that's our focus, to assist buyers to get a great deal for themselves), then as a seller for those wishing to also sell items.

You will notice that I refer mostly to vehicles, dirt bikes etc. as that is what I have dealt in mostly for the last 10 years. But these principles can be applied to anything you wish to buy or sell new or used, as I have used these principals in all of my buying and selling of all my items for years now.

I include examples and some stories from my experiences to show you how you can use the skills I am teaching you. We have made this information basic so that these skills can be applied by anyone in the world.

For legality sake I have to add that we wrote this book for information purposes only and that we take no risk or liability in what anyone chooses to do with this information and the outcomes of using this information.

Buying and selling is an art that can be learned by anyone but is a win and lose game. I have both won, lost and broken even multiple times. This game is unpredictable. But with the information and skills I am about to teach you, your chances of coming out on top are much better than before you decided to read this book.

But enough about all that, it's time to start giving you the basics, so let's begin…

Chapter One

Research: To skip this step is to fail

Research can be for some a very boring task but it is a vital and necessary part of the buying and selling process. If you haven't done your research as a buyer or seller you will surely have issues trying to get a good deal on your item.

Another reason you need to do your research is that it will aid you in all steps of the buying and selling process from start to finish. That is why we say to skip this step is to fail.

How this will help you is that you will know what other items of similar nature are going for in your area, and can use them as examples when dealing directly with the seller, especially when negotiating on the price. (We will get more into this in our negotiating chapter.)

We will first go through research for a buyer and then follow up with research for the seller, but these points are great to know for whichever aspect you choose as it gives insight into the workings of both sides.

If you want to sell an item you need to know what a buyer is looking for, and how they may have prepared ahead of time before they even contact you. So it is best to read through the entire book for the best insight and information.

Research for the Buyer

For whatever you are looking to purchase, there will be similar or the same items out there in your area being sold for different prices by different sellers, whether privately or commercially. You need to compare these prices in order to know what a "good deal" is.

Aspects you need to keep in mind are year or how old the item is, rarity, make, model, condition, options you must or need the item to have and compare items with the same aspects and options only.

If you are looking at vehicles, sleds, dirt bikes, quads etc., and the option is there, then mileage or running hours are a must know to compare with similar items.

Most people make the mistake of not taking these factors into account, and that is where you get into trouble. You also must remember not to judge an item by how "pretty" it is (I know it's hard) as some of the nicest looking items can have more problems than you can, or want, to deal with.

Most people know that mileage on a car, truck, SUV or van is important, but most don't know what a good mileage range is on other items. So, do your research, and if you don't know a great tip is to call a place that repairs the item and ask them. This is because they specialize in repair and they can *usually* tell you what "high mileage" for that item is.

Based on the information on the item from the details above you will be able to find the average going price for that item.

TIP: Make sure you are looking at the prices of the items within your area as location does play a factor on the price.

For example: An item priced in Alberta, Canada, where there are less of that item than say in Ontario, Canada, is usually higher in price than the same item in Ontario, Canada, where the market contains countless numbers more of that item. This is because the population is much higher in that province and more of that item would be sold in that area, so more exist naturally brining the price for that item down.

You also need to know that the prices of items and amount of negotiation room on the price differ greatly depending on who is selling them. A dealer for instance may have less room to move on the price versus a private seller or vice versa.

Another factor to remember is how long the item has been for sale, as those who have just started advertising versus those who have had it advertised for a long amount of time, will differ in how much they are willing to take for the item. (We will get more into this in the following chapters.)

You also need to evaluate your skill set when looking to purchase an item. What we mean is that if you can fix an item, then you may be able to get a better deal, as a broken version of the item you are looking for will be much cheaper than one in full working condition (also referred to as turn-key).

This is one of the ways I have been successful when buying items, as I have the ability to fix, or learn to fix the item due to my previous skill set. And anyone can do this; it just takes time, practice and a particular interest in an area that drives you like a hobby would.

If you are not able to fix the item yourself, you may still be able to purchase an item in a state that needs repairs, as you may personally know someone who can fix the item and you can get it done cheaper and still come in lower than the price of an item that is turn-key.

TIP: If you know someone that can fix the item you are looking at, find out what it needs ahead of time and talk to the person that may be able to fix it. Ask them what it may cost on a low to high scale to get the item in turn-key condition, and assess if it would be more or less than buying a turn-key item.

One last factor that can aid you in getting a great deal is the time of year you are trying to buy an item. For instance, in any area with a snowy winter, you may be able to get a much better deal on a boat when there is snow on the ground versus the kickoff of summer or boating season. I try to buy snowmobiles in the summer for instance, as they are way cheaper and I can sell them for a higher price come the kickoff of winter, or the first snowfall.

Research for the Seller

As a seller, knowing what the buyer is taking into account when shopping for an item such as yours, gives you insight into how to sell your item. That is why we say regardless of your plan to buy or sell read this entire book for both sides of the business.

Even a seller needs to do their research to make sure they are pricing their item so that it will sell and so they are knowledgeable for the buyer when they are asking about the item in comparison to other similar items.

The first thing you need to do is assess what you are selling in a similar way the buyer will be assessing your item. You need to look at the year or how old the item is, make, model, mileage or hours if applicable and the overall condition.

You also need to *sometimes* take into consideration what you have into the item. The reason I say *sometimes* is because you may have bought the item new many years ago, and it has devalued over time, or because sometimes when the item was bought, we are sorry to say, but you may have paid top dollar or too much for it.

You must be honest with yourself in order to price your item in a way that is competitive, and you must look at the market value within your items assessment range in order to price your item. You can take into account in your price some recent maintenance or repair costs for new parts, but keep in mind that no matter what you have done to the item, it is still the same item.

For Example: If you put $10,000 into a Ford Tempo for say new paint, some parts and a fancy stereo system, it won't matter when it comes to selling the car, it is still just a Ford Tempo. Some items become more valuable the more money you put into them, like a classic car for example, but most items stay the same regardless of how much money you put into them. Even some classic car owners lose money because regardless of what you spend, there is still a top value on most items, and if you spend more than that top value amount, you will not get all of your money you have invested into the item back.

TIP: If you want to sell your item quickly then you need to stick to the lower end of your price range or do what I usually do, and price it a bit lower than the average so mine sells first.

You also need to research the best avenue with which to sell your item in your area. You want to choose the avenue with the most readerships, and that will get the most traffic. Every area has different methods such as online listings, newspapers, and bulletin boards, and it may take some trial and error to find what works best for you.

A big factor you need to consider is also the time of year you are selling. There are certain times of the year that selling certain items will fetch you a better dollar than other times. For instance, if you want to sell a boat then you need to hit peak season, which is in the early spring. If you get too far into the summer you will have a very hard time selling the boat, and any other time of the year it will fetch hundreds if not thousands less than peak season. So make sure you are selling your item at the "kick off" of its peak season.

Also take into account if the item may be desirable as a gift near certain holidays and start trying to sell it during the "buying" time for those looking to purchase items as gifts. This may also help your item sell for a better dollar if it is a desirable holiday gift item.

The most important aspect of selling an item is honesty, both with yourself and your buyer. Some believe it's better to hide issues with the item and hope a buyer doesn't notice in order to get a better price, but this can come back to haunt you in several ways.

Remember that the person you are selling to may have your phone number, address, name etc. and can create havoc in your life when they start finding the issues you left out or tried to hide.

Regardless of what the issues are with your item there will usually be someone out there looking to buy an item like yours, which is willing and able to fix the item if the price is based fairly taking the issues into account.

So just be honest and upfront with people to save yourself the stress, grief and headache in the future. It will also aid in your sale to point out the issues, and we will get more into that later in the book.

Selling an item is a very personal thing and if your honest with yourself and others, and do the proper research, the experience will go more smoothly and positively.

Now that you know all about the first step in buying and selling, let's get into the advertising information for both what to look for as buyers, and how best to advertise as sellers.

Chapter Two

Advertising: Reading between the lines

Some people are a natural at advertising but others are a bit more awkward when it comes to this skill. When we first started out I was the awkward one, meanwhile my girlfriend used to write all the ads as she was better with words and this skill.

Even as a buyer you may have a need to advertise for what you are looking for so take the time to read this entire chapter so that you know both buying and selling advertising skill sets.

During the research stage we just went over you will be going through ads to see how much others are asking for the items you are looking to purchase. When you are looking through the ads there are many indicators you will be looking for to determine if the value is accurate and may be negotiable.

Now, even though this will seem like a lot to look for, with time and practice, you will be able to see all of the following information quickly and effectively while scanning ads. So don't worry, it's not as time consuming as it will seem at first.

An ad is both the buyer and sellers first impression, and if done correctly can get the attention of a potential buyer right away and get them interested and excited about the item, but it can also do the complete opposite.

As a buyer or seller you will need to know what to look for in an ad that will help you with the buying and selling process, and give you a peek into the advertisers circumstances, personality etc.

So let's break down the factors you want to look for in ads for buyers and sellers.

Ad reading for buyers

The first thing most ads will usually feature is a picture of the item, and most times that will draw your attention before anything else like the title or information.

The first thing you need to understand about pictures is that with technology these days, anyone can produce a nice clear picture of their item, so you need to be careful. Most pictures will show an item as being in much nicer condition than it actually is in person so keep this in mind.

Another problem with pictures is that a seller can hide defects on an item by taking pictures at the right angle, or feature many pictures on the ad like they are being transparent, but neglect to take pictures at all sides "forgetting" the worst part of the item, and essentially hiding the biggest problem areas.

Also beware if you see a lot of pictures, but there is one side that is missing. When a seller is taking the time to post that many pictures, they are being thorough, and sometimes (albeit rarely) they may have legitimately forgot that one angle in the process. But my experience has proven otherwise, in that most of the time, it is because they are purposefully hiding something.

You also need to beware if they post only one picture, especially if that one picture is at a bad or far away angle, where you are unable to see most of the item. This usually also indicates that they are hiding something, as bad pictures such as this usually indicates a dishonest or lazy seller. The item may be in a lot worse condition than they are letting on.

Another way sellers may hide the condition of the item is to put a picture that is the same item in great condition (also called a "stock photo") and then they put in the ad that it is not a picture of their item, but that their item looks the same. Well "looks the same" can mean many different things to many different people, so even though most times this is not the case, technically they are being honest in a dishonest way, so you should just steer clear.

All of these tactics some sellers use is where that honesty factor comes into play, and right off this is a bad impression for you the buyer. These tactics are meant to draw a buyer out to see the item, in hopes that in person they can overlook the imperfections and still buy the item. This is a very dishonest move that should make you wonder what else they are hiding. It's better to just steer clear of ads such as this where the seller is being dishonest or trying in a roundabout way to deceive you.

The next item in an ad you will look at is the title of the ad and there are too many variables to list off, so just use your judgement. Some people try to be funny, some try to put as much info as possible in the title and some use it to catch your attention. The title is not as important as the body of the ad itself, which is our next point we are going to cover.

In the body of the ad before the seller writes out their pitch about their item you may find a basic list of information, usually near the top, that they could fill out when posting their item, as well as information that may automatically be there such as listing date. This is mostly for online ads on free or paid online sites.

All information in the ads is important so you should look at all information provided and read the entire ad. Let's break down some of the information you may see, and how it can help you in many ways.

The first point you may see could be the date the ad was posted and/or edited last. This is important because it will give you an indication of how long the item has been posted for sale.

With this information you can perceive how negotiable a person may be, as the longer it takes to sell the item, the more willing to negotiate they may be. It also works the opposite way because if they have recently started to advertise then they will sometimes want to wait and see what other "bites" they get on their item, and are sometimes less willing to negotiate. (We will go into more detail on this later in the book.)

The next point you may see is the price, which is great if they fill that in, but sometimes they may put in a "dummy" number like "$12345" or a "please contact", "make an offer" or "swap/trade". Anything other than the price can be frustrating for a buyer, and is counterproductive for the seller, as many buyers won't bother with the ad or item if they have to dig for a price.

Personally I mostly do the same as others and skip on past these ads, because my view is that if you aren't willing to put a price upfront, then you aren't motivated to sell your item. You may choose to do some digging to get a price if you really want the item, but beware as these individuals are sometimes searching for a "bidding war" to see how much (or what else in a trade) they can get for their item. Generally, if they can't be upfront on their price, then they are already wasting your time by making you dig for an answer.

Next, how the person talks about their item in their ad, is as important as the length of their ad, and the amount of information contained in the ad about their item. You want to look out for ads with both too much and/or too little information. The amount and quality of information can tell you a lot about the item and the seller.

If a seller is serious about selling their item they will provide enough important information without going overboard. The sellers who provide an overload of information are trying way too hard to upsell their item, which means they are trying to distract you from the issues the item may have by telling you every little good feature the item contains.

We all know that cars have wheels, a steering wheel and windows, or at least they should, so why are you getting a huge list of the basics the item always contains? What are they trying to hide and what are they not telling you?

On the opposite side of the information spectrum you may want to steer clear of ads that provide little to no information. The seller either doesn't care about selling their item, or they don't have much to say because their item may not be in the greatest condition.

Sometimes sellers are vague in their ads because they are trying to hide issues or defects, kind of like the term "if you can't say anything nice, don't say anything at all", and they hope no one notices. But now you will take notice because you are reading this book.

Sellers will also try to use their wording to slyly make you believe the item is fine, so you need to read between the lines. Some will also outright lie about their item, or use wording to make you believe the item is fine, then in the next line give you an indication that it isn't.

For Example: *"The vehicle runs and drives great! It is very reliable and lady driven."* (Which really doesn't matter by the way when they say lady driven, I have seen both men and women drive their vehicle hard.) Then later in the ad it says…blah, blah, blah… *"needs motor."* OR somewhere in the ad it may say *"Runs and rives great, needs starter."*

You may be laughing right now, but this is a common type of ad I see almost daily, and these are real examples of actual ads I have seen. You have to ask yourself "how can it run and drive great, but also has an issue such as needing a motor? What is really wrong with the item?" Steer clear of these types of ads as they will surely cost you in the end.

Make sure you always read the entire ad as some of the most important information is usually at the bottom of the ad. Some people only read the first part of an ad and miss the most important info, such as the state the item is currently in or when and how the seller would like to be contacted.

We have had so many people call and ask us questions about items we have advertised in which the ad has answered, if they had just read the entire ad. I have gotten to the point with these people that I will ask if they read the entire ad and tell them to go back and read it and then call me back.

After so long in the buying and selling business I just don't have the time to deal with people who can't even bother to read the entire ad on an item they are supposedly interested in. Call me a jerk but it really boils down to a difference between a serious buyer and a "tire kicker". We will cover the different types of buyers and sellers you may encounter later in this book and how to tell the difference.

It is sometimes hard to weed out the bad ads compared to the good ones, you just need to read between the lines and ask lots of questions if you choose to contact someone with one of these types of ads. (We will go into this more in the initial contact section of this book.)

The next item you will need to check on an ad, if it has it, will be the amount of visits the ad has gotten. This can be an indicator of many factors including if there may be more issues with the item than the seller is letting on.

What we mean is if the item has been posted for a somewhat short period of time and has a lot of visits, the price is then usually in a decent range, but why hasn't it sold yet? The reason may be because there are more issues with the item than they are letting on, causing people who call or go see the item to walk away.

On the other hand, if there aren't very many visits, and the item has been posted for a long period of time, then the price is most likely set too high for anyone to even bother going as far as reading the ad, let alone going to see the item. The ad may also be poorly done causing people to just skip on by.

The above examples are not always the case that may be affecting people not buying or not looking at ads, as location of the seller can also play into a buyers decisions. If you live outside of a main centre, it is much harder to motivate people to take the drive to buy an item. That can sometimes be the reason the seller has less visits or still has the item after a long period of time, but has a lot of visits.

You also need to see how the best way to contact the seller is on the ad, as that can not only play a role in why the item hasn't sold, but also how easy it will be for you to buy the item.

The first form of contact is of course a phone number, which is the easiest, best and swiftest form of contact...that is if the person answers. (More on that later in this book). If there is a phone number, and the seller has not stated otherwise in their ad, always use this method of contact FIRST. But let me be clear, and this is very important, unless otherwise instructed by the seller to do so, CALL the number...DO NOT TEXT!

We have gotten lazy in this day and age, and are starting to use text as a form of contact instead of just dialing the number and physically talking to the person on the other end. You may be able to get by with family, friends and the odd seller with this method, but I can tell you from first-hand experience that this is a major pet peeve of sellers alike, that a serious buyer can't just pick up the phone and call for more information. You don't want to be the bad first impression and start off on the wrong foot with the seller, so make sure you contact them physically by phone (unless otherwise requested).

A seller may put contact types and time frames in their ad other than just their phone number so make sure to read the ad fully. Some of these types may be to contact them by phone (this can be either call, text or leave a message stated for this type), or e-mail. The seller may also give a time frame in which they would like to be contacted. Make sure to always use the method of contact they ask for and that it is during the time frame they ask for if applicable. There is *nothing* more disrespectful to a seller at this point, than not being contacted about *their* item in the manner which works for *them*!

The last item we will cover when looking at ads is a feature only some online sites may have but that can make a great difference on whether you choose to contact that particular seller let alone buy an item from them. This is a feature that connects the buyers email to all of the ads they have posted. It may say "view posters other ads" or "other ads by this poster" and can be a clickable link that shows you all of the ads they have posted.

Why this is helpful is that it can help you to see a bit into who the person is that is selling. If they are a dealer then obviously they will have many similar ads so that is a given and they usually advertise under their dealer name so they are easy to spot. What we are talking about at this point is a private seller.

If a private seller has many ads with similar items, or items along the same line you must proceed with caution. These types of sellers are what we like to call "curbers" and they are some of the biggest liars out there. They may also have ads looking to buy similar items as well as selling them which makes them even easier to spot.

Curbers buy cheap, sell high and do as little as possible to move the item they are selling in order to make the most profit. They know very little about the item they are selling as they usually haven't had it very long before posting it. They will usually tell you they have had it awhile, they are selling cause they bought a new one or don't need it etc. They have a million excuses they use and are only about the bottom line. They don't care who they screw over, just how much money they make in the process.

It is best to steer clear of these types of sellers so that you aren't buying an item that is a bushel of unknown issues and that may be a "money pit". There's a reason the seller got it so cheap in the first place, and you can guarantee they didn't put much money in it and fix it all up before selling it, that would take away from their bottom line...profit.

This may seem like an overwhelming amount of information and that we are making most sellers out to be thieves and crooks, but in reality there are some okay sellers out there. The biggest piece of information to remember above all else is that everyone lies, so you need to do your research and read between the lines.

You also will need to make a decision based on what you see and know with the item, to make an informed decision on whether to spend your hard earned money and get what you think is a fair deal.

We will be covering more about what to look for when you see the item in person later in this book for you to be able to put it all together and make a decision on the item to buy.

Now we will move on to some information for the seller, or buyer looking to advertise to find an item in the next section.

Advertising for Sellers

If you would like to sell an item you will need to know how to make a great ad and some tips and tricks on how to get the attention your ad deserves. If you would like to advertise as a buyer looking for an item you will also learn a lot from this information.

After you have done your research and know all about your item and how best to price it you are now ready to advertise your item. But the first thing you need to know right now is whether you for sure want to sell the item and are ready to part with it.

Believe it or not but we have come across people when trying to buy items that have not only decided during initial contact that they don't want to really sell their item, but even in person. This is a huge waste of time for all parties involved so please make sure you are ready to part with your item for sure before you advertise it.

Now that you know that you are ready to sell your item, you need to find the avenue for advertising that best suits your needs and is the quickest avenue to get your item sold. This could be online, a newspaper ad, an ad on a bulletin board etc. This is seller's choice and was part of your research to find the best method of advertising for you.

Now that you know where you will be advertising we will get into all the aspects your buyer will be looking at in order to want to contact you on your item.

The first item they will see is your main featured picture if your means of advertising has this option. So make sure you are using your nicest picture as the main one in order to get their attention.

As we mentioned in the buyers section of this book for advertising, a picture is worth a thousand words. Take the time to take good pictures to show off your item including its defects as they will see them eventually, especially if the buyer goes as far as meeting you to see the item in person. Remember to be honest and don't try to hide the good or bad that your item has, as it is what it is and you should have taken all of this into account when deciding how to price your item in the research stage of this book.

You also don't need to go overboard when taking pictures, just make sure you get as much of the item as you can, usually a good number is between 2 and 6 pictures. If you go overboard it will seem like you are trying too hard to sell your item and may hurt your chances of having a serious buyer contact you. A buyer may ask for more pictures so you can send them the ones you didn't post then.

Another feature of a picture you will need to take into account is background. This is important not only for making sure to feature the item in a great way but also for your protection. Keep the background as plain as you can and make sure you are not giving strangers and thieves a peek into your personal life.

What we mean is that if you have a vehicle near the item then it may have the license plate number showing. Or if you take a picture in your garage you may be giving everyone a look at all the other items of value that are in there.

Also if you take a picture outside your house make sure your address isn't visible so you aren't giving away your location to everyone. You want to be able to control who shows up at your house and when, especially if you live in a higher crime area.

It is your private space and you need to make sure it is safe for you and your family so always review your pictures in detail before posting them online and check the background. Having to take new pictures is much easier than the alternative of theft, etc., so please be careful.

The next part of an ad you may need is a title especially for most online ads. This is your first impression on a buyer so make sure it's a good one. This may not make or break your ad for some to look at it but it can make an impact on whether a potential buyer will want to look further and actually continue into and read your ad.

The best title is one that gives information for what you are selling such as year, make, model, drive type etc. These title spaces are usually a low amount of characters so you will need to be short and concise.

For Example: 1994 Chevrolet Tahoe 4x4 SUV for sale

Try not to be funny or vague about what you are selling in the title as most will just skip past your ad to one that actually gives some information about what is being sold. The world seems to be in a hurry these days so you need to catch people's attention in a minimum amount of characters.

The last tip we will cover about the title is to make sure you know what you are selling and that the spelling and information is correct. There's no better way to make people skip past your ad than to make yourself look like an idiot by listing an item that doesn't exist or that you can't spell. This makes you look uninformed and frankly stupid, and will kill your sale before it even starts.

For many online ads you will have a list of information options you can fill out for your ad and this is a great way to give as much information as you can before the buyer even gets to the body of your ad. It is best to take the time and fill the information out the best you can as it makes it easier for the buyer to get vital points about your item right off the bat.

When you get to the description or body of the ad, this is now your time to make your item shine in comparison to others alike. This is what makes a person want to contact you for your item. Beware that it can also turn people away if done incorrectly.

First off you want to make sure that all the information that a person is looking for about your item is there without going overboard. Just think about the basic points you would want to know about the item first and list them off.

Keep it simple and to the point, and make sure your spelling is correct and the ad makes sense. People hate reading long drawn out ads of textbook style information, but they also don't want to see a tiny ad with little to no information as that means more work for them.

When it comes to an address that is shown in the ad we recommend only putting a general location such as the city you live in. The reason for this is similar to the point we covered about backgrounds of pictures, it is for your safety and protection.

Unfortunately in this day and age there are people that can be either a bit crazy or thieves, and you don't want anyone showing up at your house whenever they want or in the middle of the night to steal from you. Keep yourself and your family safe by not advertising where you live along with your item.

Now some of you may think "well I have to get people to come to my

home/work to get the item and they need to know where I live, right?".
Yes this is true, but they don't need to know until the right time so you
can be protected, and we will go over when the right time is in a later
chapter.

You also need to figure out the way you would like to be contacted for
someone to purchase your item. The best form of contact if you are able
to do it is by phone number.

Only put your phone number in the ad if you are willing to be contacted
in that manner and can answer it. If you are unable to answer your phone
until say the evening then put your number if you like, but stipulate in
your ad the time frame that is best to get a hold of you. Don't forget some
people may miss that time frame in your ad and call outside your time
frame.

If you put your number in the ad but don't answer your phone or call
people back when they leave a message then you will be killing your sale,
so only put a number in for calls if you are able to answer the calls.

Other methods that you can use your phone, but not have to answer it,
can be to have it stipulated in your ad for the buyers to text or leave a
message. Just remember that some people won't read that far into the ad
to get that message and will just call. This is why we stress to read the
entire ad in our buyers section above!

The last form of contact we will cover is by email. This is more
convenient and easy if you use an online ad service, as it is usually
connected directly to your email, and there is usually a reply box for the
buyer to reply to your ad. If you don't want to be contacted in any other
way than emails, make sure you don't put your number in the ad and the

buyer will have no other option than to email you.

There are benefits and drawbacks to each way of contact but I would say that email only is the one form that will turn people away from your ad the most and hurt your sale.

People like to be able to get a hold of a seller right away as they are in the moment and excited about the item. If they do go as far as emailing you (which is probably 50-50 that they will go that far) then they expect a timely response. If you drag your feet in getting back to people they may have forgotten about your item, lost interest or already found one elsewhere to buy and you lose a potential sale.

When you choose email you must also remember that those who responded to your item first should get first option so you must go to the bottom of your replies in your email, not the top as that is how most email sorts in most inboxes, the top is most recent emails not the first ones you received.

TIP: If you have a phone number some people will be lazy and just email you. In this case they are most likely not a serious buyer and just wasting your time if you have a better means they can contact you with. We don't even respond to such people anymore as it is always a waste of time we have found.

The last point we will finish this topic of ads with is: ad view, number of calls and amount of email responses. All of these items are tied together and we will explain why.

Some online ad sites have an ad viewed number for how many times your ad has been looked at. We touched on how this number can help a buyer to find out a bit more information about the seller, but it has a different meaning for you the seller.

This also ties into your responses from potential buyers in whichever means you have chosen by phone in some way or by email. The amount of calls, emails, texts and views you receive from your ad are not as important as the people who are actually willing to meet you and view your item.

There are many factors that can influence the numbers of views and responses, but the important part you need to focus on is the serious potential buyer who will actually show up with the intent to truly buy. We will get into more detail on how to tell and what not to do in the following chapters.

Since you have now learned about the first two aspects of research and advertising for the buying and selling world we will now cover the initial contact for buyers and sellers.

Chapter Three

Initial Contact: Play nice or pay the price

For some people this is a hard step to take especially if they have not done their research and if they don't know what they are looking for in ads. Some people also have a hard time contacting and talking with strangers especially when they are looking for a deal.

In this part of the book we will cover the basics on how to make initial contact for both buyers and sellers to try to help this step go smoother for both parties involved.

There are very few people out there who are completely comfortable with contacting buyers and sellers alike on their ads like I am, so this chapter will really help you to know what to do and what not to do in both aspects.

We will first teach all of you buyers out there the basics you need to know.

Initial Contact for Buyers

After you have done your research and found an ad for a seller you wish to contact, how do you make the first move to contact them?

Well, first you need to make sure you have read the entire ad and know the means in which the seller would like to be contacted as we mentioned in the previous chapter. Once you have established the best route in which to contact them you need to do some preparation before you do.

When you read over the ad there should have been some unanswered questions that came to mind. If not, you should read the ad again and really make sure there's no information missing that you would like to know about the item before you make the steps to go see the item in person.

There has been very few times in my experience that there hasn't been at least one more piece of information that I needed in order to decide whether or not to actually make the move to go and view, and potentially purchase an item. So if you have done your research ahead of time you should have some questions for the seller that they did not answer for you in the ad.

If you know the questions you need to ask I would suggest writing them down if you are calling the seller as you will most likely forget them during the frenzy of the call. It is not only embarrassing to call the seller multiple times with more questions, but can hurt you for negotiations later when they believe you are inexperienced at buying or don't know much about what they are selling.

Now you are ready to contact the seller, and in these points we are going to mostly use the best and most used contact method, a phone call. We will also be sure to explain the differences when needed for the other methods of contact.

If you make the call and no one answers, show the seller you are serious by leaving a message stating your first name, what you are calling about and leave a phone number they can contact you with. You may call again that day if you wish but only leave one message, and I wouldn't call more than 3 times in a day, most of us have caller ID and can see how many times you are calling. You don't want to appear desperate.

Now let's get into what to do if they answer, or when they call you back.

The first rule of thumb is to always be polite and courteous no matter how the seller talks to you. Use "yes sir/ma'am, no sir/ma'am", "please and thank you", and other respectful terms while dealing with the seller. Remember that the seller may have already been dealing with "idiots" and "tire-kickers" trying to sell their item so they may be more abrasive during initial contact than they may be in person.

Once they realize you are a serious buyer unlike the others they have had to deal with, the seller will generally loosen up and release the more abrasive attitude towards you. Being rude and disrespectful will not get you anywhere closer to the item or making a great deal.

One quick note before we break down the conversation, make sure the person you are talking to is the owner of the item that is being sold and that they are of adult age in your area. If it is a minor, you can still buy the item but you must ask to talk to their parent or guardian and you need the parent or guardian to fill out the bill of sale or oversee the process depending on your local laws which we will cover more on in further chapters. Just to be safe if you don't know your local laws, always try to have the parent or guardian involved in the process to prevent problems later.

Now, let's break down a general conversation for this initial contact and how it should go.

After you are met with your general greeting such as "Hello" introduce yourself to the seller and let them know why you are calling. "Hi, my name is "YOUR FIRST NAME" and I am calling about your "INSERT ITEM" you have for sale, do you still have it? Now that they know what the call is about it is now time to get more information and ask your questions. Remember that time is a factor for both parties involved so even though you need answers try to be short and sweet.

Once you have your questions answered and if you are satisfied with the answers and are interested in viewing the item, you can ask them when you may be able to view it. Always ask them when they are available first as it is the respectful thing to do. Just because you are excited and may be available to run and get it right now doesn't mean they are available. Everyone's lives, jobs and availability are different.

The best way to show you are serious is to say "I am interested in coming to take a look at the item right away, when would you be available to show it to me?" Try to work around their schedule and the more serious and knowledgeable you sound, the more likely they will be available to show it to you quickly.

Once you have set a time and date, ask them their name, and what the best way to contact them is in case of getting lost, running late etc. This also shows you are serious and responsible putting their mind at ease that you will show or call them if you aren't coming. If for some reason you change your mind, are running late, or can't make it CALL THEM! There is nothing worse than waiting around for a no call, no show buyer and will ruin your chances of ever buying that item from them if you choose to in the future. We will go more into this later in the book.

Once you get in the swing of using the info in this entire book you may also ask during this initial contact what the lowest price they are willing to take for their item is. It takes practice to swing this into the conversation naturally and easily so don't worry if you forget or don't feel comfortable asking just yet, this can be done face to face and we will go into more detail on that part in our negotiations portion of this book.

You will need to make a decision on whether you are interested in going to see the item on initial contact or will need more time to decide.

If you need to think more about buying the item before you set up a time to meet etc. be honest and let them know you need to think about it after you ask your questions, and give them a time frame. You could say for example " I am very interested in your item but I need to think about it, if it's ok I will call you back in "SAID TIME FRAME (5 minutes, an hour, tomorrow)" and let you know either way."

Make sure you follow through with this agreement just in case for some reason you decide to purchase the item at a later date, even if initially you decided against it. You must remember that most people have caller ID so if you mess them around now you will ruin your chances later at purchasing their item if you change your mind.

There are benefits and drawbacks to thinking about the item and getting back to people. The most I would go is 5 to 15 minutes to discuss it with my girlfriend and I tell them that. People understand if you need to discuss the purchase of your item with your significant other and will usually give you that time. But you could miss out on the item if it is a good deal by waiting, also there is a risk that suddenly they may not answer their phone when you call back for whatever reason and you lose out on the item.

The rule of thumb I go by is trying to make the decision while asking my questions on whether I want the item for sure or not so I don't miss my chance to buy the item while I have the seller on the phone. It's also best to discuss the item with your significant other ahead of time before you make the contact so you know where you stand before contacting the seller. But this takes practice and quick thinking, something that will develop over time. If you have done your research and read between the lines with the ad then you should already have an idea with your questions which answers will be a deal breaker or which will clarify for you wanting to buy, for both you and any others involved such as your significant other.

During initial contact you will need to do the same as when you read the sellers ad and read between the lines. People always have a tendency to stretch the truth or outright lie. This doesn't mean they are bad people, sometimes it's because they really need the money so they are doing everything they feel is necessary to sell their item the fastest and for the most money.

This doesn't matter as much if you are following the steps in our book and making sure you are basing your assessment on what you see with the information and when you view the item. And remember, worst case scenario, you can always walk away from the item when you are viewing it in person. Making a meeting to view the item is not a commitment to buy, just a promise that you are serious about buying the item. We will go into more detail on this later for when you view the item.

If you are texting for your initial contact (of course only if it is at the sellers request would you be texting, remember?) there are some rules that are a bit different than if you were talking by phone. The basics are essentially the same; the biggest difference is that you must engage in the conversation in a timely manner as if you were on the phone. If you text the seller and they get back to you right away, or when they do get back to you, then you need to engage right away. Don't make the seller wait all day for a response, take the time and focus until the conversation is done just like you would on the phone.

Also make sure, just like you would on the phone, to talk courteously, respectfully and completely. Make sure you're not using text slang and that your texts make sense, are spelled correctly and concise. Imagine that it is a phone conversation with a potential employer, not a friend/ family conversation and that it matters what you say and how you say it.

When texting you will need to ask each question separately or the seller may miss a question as they may forget all the questions you asked previously. Because of this make sure not to play 20 questions and take a lot of the sellers time, ask your most important questions only, you can always ask the rest of your less important questions in person.

I would also suggest trying to talk to the person on the phone at some point before you set up a meeting as you never know who you are talking to on the other end of a text. It could be a child or teenager for all you know.

When emailing at the sellers request or if they have no other contact but email you can lay most out on the line if you choose, but will run the risk once again like texting of unanswered questions as they may miss or forget certain questions. The best method for email is expressing your interest and asking them to give you a call and leaving your number in the email you are sending to them. This shows that you are a serious buyer and will open it up to the above conversation structure when they make contact.

You can also request them to call you, or ask them to send you a number you can contact them with. This gives them an out if they have some issues with shyness and making the first move. So basically, don't just send your number and wait, ask for theirs as well.

With email you must remember that sometimes people forget that the top received emails in their inbox are the most recently received, not the first emails they are getting on their item, so they tend to work top down in reading and replying. If you haven't heard back I would send another email every 24 hours at the most in case they haven't gotten down to your email, just don't go all spam like sending multiples and looking like a stalker or crazy person instead of a serious buyer.

Email responses can be fast nowadays as most people have them linked to their smartphone, but sometimes you will have a seller that posts an ad and doesn't check or respond back to emails for weeks. Because of this I don't have as much confidence in an email only seller and don't put much stock in getting their item specifically. If you are looking for a fairly rare item you may be stuck with this type of seller as your only option temporarily, so keep trying to get in contact with them but in the meantime try to seek out another source for your item.

Initial contact can be stressful sometimes, but can become easy and natural the more you do it just like anything else. Just remember that they can't see you and don't know you therefore you can be more bold than in person. Don't worry as much with this stage about messing up your chances at a good deal because the majority is done in the negotiations stage while you are looking at the item.

As long as you are polite, respectful and follow through to the meeting in person portion of this event, you have set a great foundation to be successful in your buying experience.

Initial contact for Sellers

As a seller you are in control of every step in this process. It is important to remember that it is your item, your price, and that you're in the driver's seat. But this is a lot of responsibility and so far you have been doing all your work behind the scenes.

Depending on the form of communication you chose depends on how much response you will get as we went through the benefits and drawbacks in the last chapter. Whatever it is you have chosen you will need to make sure you are on top of the responses.

Now is when the fun starts, getting interest for your item from potential buyers. But this is also where the research stage comes in handy as buyers will ask you questions about your item and you will need to have the answers ready in your head. The biggest answer in your mind you will need is on the price.

Most people will ask you what your "bottom line" on your item is and this is where you need to be smart. Take some money off your price to show you are negotiable, but leave yourself some wiggle room as most buyers will try to get you to an even lower price in person during negotiations, and I will elaborate more on that in the negotiations chapter.

This may seem a bit scary to some already but as long as you know your item and are honest and open with buyers it will be easier and less stressful.

It can be somewhat frustrating trying to sell an item today and there will be times you will want to throw in the towel. People will waste your time, "tire kickers" will appear and people will show interest…then lose interest. This is a given in the selling world and is mostly unavoidable. We will get into reading people more in the later chapters to help avoid some of these frustrating scenarios.

But for now let's just say that despite what's going on with your sale, each new person that calls you is a new potential buyer so be polite and honest with each one, as the last person that may have wasted your time was not the new potential buyer's fault.

If you chose contact by phone then you will need to keep yourself available and try to answer the phone when it rings, as you can quickly lose a sale if you don't answer the calls. Some people keep their numbers blocked and/or won't leave a message making it impossible to call them back, thus you could be potentially losing a sale if they decide not to contact you again because you didn't answer the first time.

Also you want to catch people in the moment they are excited and wanting to buy, as this can quickly pass and they will change their mind. Think of every interested prospect like the person standing in line at the supermarket. They have racks near the registers with random items that a person is most likely to impulse buy if they are left waiting and looking around. But keep the line moving and they won't even bat an eye. You want to catch them in the moment as unlike the supermarket scenario; if you keep them waiting they will lose interest and move on.

If you do miss a call and receive a message then you need to return their call ASAP or risk losing a potential sale. In this day and age things move very quickly and people will move on to the next similar item right away. They will take whoever is available first and most likely buy the next guys item if they get immediate response and can get to the item physically quickly.

If you choose text as your form of contact the same rules apply as the phone contact. Be available and respond immediately for your best chance at selling your item quickly.

And with emails you must check them frequently and respond back as soon as you can. Remember with emails to start from the bottom of the new messages in your inbox as in reality those were your first responders and it is only fair (with most email inboxes, if unsure check the time the email was received).

Yes, no one will actually know but you, but that's not being fair and honest now is it. Also a better way to get your emails quickly is to connect them through your smartphone, then you will get them easily and quickly in order to respond to your potential buyers.

You must be available and ready to respond once your ad is out there for the best chance of success. You must also be available to show the item, because if you are out of town, or don't have time to show the item to potential buyers, there's no point in advertising the item. You will just be pushing away potential sales by delaying when you can show the item. This may seem like common sense but I have come across so many ads of people doing exactly this. This will kill your sale right away, so don't post your item until you are available to show it!

Try to be patient but stern with the buyer, even in this stage, you are in control and you want the buyer to see that as well. If the buyer wants to come and look at the item, take into account when they would like to come look at it, but your schedule is what is important. You don't want to put yourself out or look desperate. If when they ask to come look at it doesn't work for you then say so, and try to come to a mutual agreement.

You also need to feel out the buyer to see how serious they are, or if they may just be wasting your time. I have encountered so many sellers who are stuck holding their item for days or weeks for someone who said they were coming to buy it "for sure". This causes a loss in sales for people because 9 times out of 10 that person will back out and there are many excuses I have heard as to why.

I myself have fallen victim at the beginning of my buying and selling experience to losing sales due to these promises. My advice here is to never hold items without a non-refundable deposit and never for more than a week. You are not Joe Bob's free storage and layaway program. I am very blunt with my "customers" and tell them first come first served...period! As should you.

I have also taken small non-refundable deposits and had to keep their money as agreed and repost my item because the buyer backed out at the last second. This can come with a lot of grief and I rarely take deposits for the simple fact that people hate losing money and I hate having to keep it. To this day it makes me feel uncomfortable and I have been in this game for about 10 years.

Honestly, as most of you are newbies to the buying and selling world I will touch on the concept of deposits, but very briefly. I highly suggest that for now you forget the concept even exists. Just stick to first come first served, until you are comfortable asking for a non-refundable deposit.

How a non-refundable deposit works is basically having the buyer secure the item for a small amount of money until they show up to buy the item. The reason they are small is because I want the amount to motivate the person, but not cost them a whole lot if they decide not to take the item. It is non-refundable because not only is it a motivator for the person to show up for the item (as promised), but it also covers some cost for your time and effort in waiting for the person to show up. It also covers the fact that during that time you may have lost potential sales if the person decides not to take the item. This is the only way now that I will "hold" an item for someone. No deposit equals first come first served on all my items.

I know it sounds cold, but after learning everything I am telling you, you will see why you need to be stern and somewhat cold as a seller. If you give anyone an inch of your control they will try to screw you over bigtime, so tough love works best for me as a teacher and you as a seller.

Other indicators that someone during initial contact will show that they are not a serious and not a potential buyer are; not wanting to view the item anytime soon or can't seem to give a time or day when they would like to come see it, nitpicking the item on the phone, asking questions that you clearly answered in the ad (because if they weren't serious enough to read the ad entirely they are not a serious buyer), and if a person contacts you by another means such as email or text when you have your number listed to call they are not just lazy but also not a serious buyer. These are just some of the basic ways you can tell someone is not a potential buyer.

For your safety, similar to when you did your ad, DO NOT reveal your exact location until they are on their way at the earliest. I have made the mistake in the past many times of giving out my home address and the potential buyer never shows, or calls, and yet now they know exactly where I live. Scary thought, so I learned quickly how to get around that scenario.

I feel out people on the phone, and sometimes if I get a bad feeling from them, I make the decision to not even let them come to my house if I don't have to. I will meet them at a busy public location like a gas station, supermarket parking lot etc. If I have no choice because the item I am selling is not easily relocatable, I hold off on giving my address until the last second. I have even turned down meetings and potential sales because I felt uncomfortable with the person I was talking to.

Always trust your gut, if something feels off don't allow that person near your home, and if you decide to meet them somewhere bring another person along (preferably another adult), even if they just sit in your vehicle.

If someone wants to come look at your item and it is something you must show from your home you must take steps to protect your home, family and yourself. You can set a time and date however do not yet give a location. If you live alone, don't tell them that and let someone know what's going on just in case. And you can always fake someone being in your home into the conversation so the person coming thinks there's someone else around in your home.

Tell the buyer to give you a call when they are ready to come look at your item and you can either pick somewhere nearby to meet them such as a gas station and have them follow you to your house or tell them to give you a call when they get to that same gas station and you will direct them from there. This way you know they are going to be there before you tell them where you live.

We will get more into the protecting yourself aspect in the next chapter but this is the setup for when you are talking to the buyer on the phone. Honestly of late I have seen some pretty horrible stories of people meeting potential buyers with events happening to either party that were potentially life threatening and you really can't be too careful. I know at times I have potentially put myself in danger meeting people for either buying or selling but I will not put my girlfriend, home or other belongings at risk for any amount of money. Just play it safe is my best advice.

You also need to be careful with your wording in the next few stages of this process starting now at the initial contact stage. The buyer will ask many questions about your item and you need to be careful with how you say things to them as much as what you say. Don't make any claims about your item that can be taken differently by the buyer than what the reality is. And be honest, it is more trouble and much harder to try to lie than to just tell the truth. During this phase it is very important to be honest so you don't waste your time or the buyers, if someone is still willing to come and view your item knowing the truth you are more likely to have a successful sale through the viewing.

For Example: Instead of saying an item runs and drives great, I would say that the last time I drove the item it ran and drove fine. You don't want to guarantee anything, or allow others to assume that's what you mean.

My last piece of information in this chapter is going to keep you from accidentally giving your item away for free later. Tell your buyer, if they have agreed on a time, date and place to meet to bring cash for the item and a way to get it home. This is important because you are weeding out some of the non-serious buyer's right here and now.

You are also setting the form of payment you will accept, cold hard CASH, there is NO OTHER FORM as safe and secure, and even cash can be iffy with counterfeiting these days. DO NOT accept any kind of cheques; I don't care if they came from the president, prime minister or Queen of England herself. DO NOT FALL FOR THIS OLD SCAM! Even an email money transfer can go sideways so CASH ONLY is your best and safest bet.

You are also letting them know that you expect them to have a way to take the item immediately. I have actually told people this and had them show up with a small car to look at a quad or dirt bike. Let's just say they thought I was a jerk because as soon as they got out of their car I have told them they wasted the drive because I am not even wasting my time showing them the item if they were not serious enough to have a way to get it home. Tough love people, you must sometimes give tough love.

If they can't show up with cash and/or a way to get your item home they are not a serious buyer...period. So don't be afraid to turn them away, you're not losing a sale because it was never there to begin with.

Now, on to the next stage in this book where you will be meeting either as a buyer, or seller in person to view the item.

Chapter Four

Meet and Greet: Let the dance begin!

In this stage we will be going over the dos and don'ts of meeting someone with the intent of an exchange of money for goods. For many people this is the most stressful part that makes both buyers and sellers want to run for the hills.

Don't be intimidated anymore, as after reading this book you will become better acquainted with this whole process and feel more confident about the meeting and negotiations stage to follow in the next chapters.

A meet and greet can be a fun and exciting experience, especially if you are more confident in your buying and selling knowledge.

After all of the information you have read in this book this stage should already feel easier since you are armed with all the knowledge about your item and know what you are looking for.

There are many similarities between the buyer and seller when it comes to the meeting stage, but we will cover both sides for a complete look at the whole spectrum.

Meet and Greet for Buyers

So you set up a time and place to meet and believe you know most of what you need to in order to make an informed decision to buy the item you are going to look at. You are a serious buyer ready to make a deal and take home the item, right?

Hold on, there are some things you need to know before we get into the negotiations and purchasing of an item and we are going to go through them all, don't worry. So let's get started on the etiquette of meeting with the seller you need to know.

First off you will need to know where and when you are meeting them which will most likely be the seller's home or work, but that's not all. You need to make sure you have the cash to buy the item, bring it with you in the full amount even though you plan on getting the item for less just in case this seller will not budge. With carrying cash and the seller knowing this, it is good to have someone, preferably and adult, with you for safety and security. There has been cases of buyers being robbed at a meet and greet location because the "seller" or thief knows they have the money on them and has set them up to rob them. So bring someone along and make sure your meeting place is as safe and public as possible.

You also need to make sure you have a way to get the item home. For instance if you are going to pick up a car, make sure you have a plate and a second driver. If your area requires paperwork to drive it home you will need to go and get that before you drive it home, so make sure you plan with enough time to go and get what you need before the place you have to get your paperwork closes.

If it is a larger item like a quad or say couch, you will need a truck or pull behind trailer of some sort large enough for the item. If you don't own one then you will need to find a way to have one at the meet and greet. The process will go much easier if you have the way to take the item immediately after buying as that is what sellers want, to have it sold and gone immediately. You don't want to have to come back for your item and either does the seller.

When you arrive at the location make sure to park legally and respectfully as this is someone's home or work. You may not have connections to their area, but they have to live or work there and don't need neighbors or coworkers mad with them because their selling of an item inconvenienced people for a while. You also don't need a ticket or accident during this transaction.

You also need to assess the area before getting out of your vehicle looking for hazards and dangers such as traffic, loose animals and dogs (especially on rural locations), a threatening amount of people like a large gathering of guys waiting for you. Your safety is priority above all else so be careful, and if it is screaming alarms at you leave the situation and walk away. Nothing is worth your life.

When you arrive and the assessment comes up as safe, always go to the door or approach the seller and introduce yourself. A firm handshake is also a valuable and respectful thing to do right off during introductions. DO NOT APPROACH THE ITEM FIRST and do not touch the item unless invited to do so! This is a very disrespectful move and will hurt your chances at a great deal immediately. The item is still owned by the seller and you must respect the seller and item.

Think of it as being in a stranger's house for the first time. You are respectful and polite and don't touch anything without being invited to.

And if you do touch something you are invited to it is always with the utmost delicacy and care. This is the same situation. The item is not yours until the deal is signed sealed and delivered so treat it with care and respect or you will sour the sellers view of you and hurt any chance you have at getting a great deal.

When the seller leads you to look at the item start a conversation about it. You can ask how long they have had it to get the ball rolling, and remember they have memories and emotional attachments to the item in most cases so that can make for great conversation about the item and even though its somewhat off topic , it can give you background history on the item. You want to get all the information you can so listen and engage the conversation, don't just make it about the item and specifics to buy it.

Talk about the item as well, ask any questions you have and get a feel for the seller's history of the item. You may think you don't have much to talk about but you have done your research and know more than you think. Compliment the item and create conversation outside of the item like you are genuinely interested, don't just focus on the item. Getting the seller talking comfortably will help you both relax and will make the negotiation process easier later.

When looking at the item find and point out any flaws or problems you notice in a non-challenging way, but also compliment the item. Point out the pros and cons of the item in a respectful manner. Be sure not to be rude or make it seem like you are insulting the seller and the item (as the two go hand in hand). Agree with what the seller is saying (in this case the seller is always right, not the customer, even if you know differently in your mind) and find common ground with them on the item.

If it is an item that requires a test drive such as a vehicle, ask if you can see it operate, and if they allow you to operate it make sure that you do not abuse the item in any way. Remember that the item is not yours yet and may never be if you decide not to purchase it so treat the item and the owner with respect.

Now that you have looked the item over, learned all you needed to learn and gotten comfortable with the seller we will go into the sellers' aspect of this section, then on to the negotiations portion of this book to try and get yourself that great deal.

Meet and Greet for the Seller

You have made the commitment to meet with a potential buyer for your item, so now what?

First of all you need to make sure you are keeping your family, home and personal property safe during this meeting if you have decided to have the buyer meet you at your house.

Try to avoid having the buyer into your home for any reason, even if they need to use the bathroom. You don't need to give a stranger a walk-through of your home and life for any reason. Especially with there being a lot of gas stations around that they can use when nature calls. If the item is in your home then make sure to take them the most direct and shortest route to the item. Don't let them get an inventory of your possessions.

If the item is in an out building such as a garage and you can swing it, take the item out and close up your shop, you can always put it back later. This is for the same reason as above. You don't need someone knowing what else you have. This prevents potential future thefts because if the rest is out of sight, it's out of mind as well.

And don't let the buyer know what else you have or where and how everything is stored. No matter how secure and safe you think your items are you must remember the old saying that locks are for honest people. If a thief wants something they will get it.

I once sold a machine to a guy that seemed honest and he came back that night and stole another machine I had which was secured. He had intended to come back again and steal another machine from me but I had figured out who it was and what happened very quickly.

He had the audacity to post ads for the items online, one being what he stole and the other being the last item I had that he hadn't stolen…yet. I wasn't able to get the original item he stole back but I was able to prevent the second item from getting stolen.

It turned out that he belonged to a large ring of thieves that was being watched and investigated by the police and had been to jail several times because of it. The point is that you never know who you are dealing with so put your safety and protection first always, you can never be too careful.

When the buyer does meet with you to look at your item make sure that you don't try to push the item on them or seem desperate to sell. Allow them to make the decision on their own while providing the information they are seeking. Make sure to still stand your ground and be stern, but in a roundabout way make it seem that you don't care to sell your item.

To gain the trust of your buyer point out the pros and cons of your item. No item is perfect and you should always be honest about the flaws so there are no surprises for them later, and therefore no problems with the buyer later either. Remember, they have some of your information and may now know where you live, so to avoid any potential problems later, be honest now.

Buyers will appreciate and respect you for your honesty, and it will only hurt the sale if the buyer wasn't serious to begin with. This is where being honest on the phone during initial contact was also important so there are no major surprises once the buyer comes to see you that could cause them to walk away.

If your item requires some sort of test drive you first need to assess whether you would be better off showing them the operation or allowing them to operate the item themselves. This is especially important when it comes to an item only some people may know how to operate such as items like a motorcycle or skid steer.

It is important to feel the person out and if you are not comfortable having them operate the item then you can do it and it will be just as effective. If you do decide to allow them to operate it and they will be leaving the property make sure to go with them, it will keep them more in line to not "bag" the item and you will know they will bring it back.

If you are going with someone on a test drive let someone know where you are going and how long you will be gone, and don't be afraid to make it obvious to the buyer that someone knows what's going on.

You may say I am being really paranoid, but I really didn't think about this either until I came across a story recently of a man who was kidnapped with his vehicle on a test drive and killed, all for the vehicle and the vehicle wasn't even anything special.

Now, on to the most important lesson of this book, negotiating for a great deal.

Chapter Five

Negotiating a deal: Easier than you think

Here we are, the moment you have all been waiting for, how to negotiate yourself a great deal and save money!

Despite what others may tell you, this is the trickiest and most unpredictable stage you will encounter. Don't believe anyone who tells you it's a simple no brainer and will always go your way because in reality that is far from the truth.

There are so many variables that can affect how well you do in this stage and I could honestly write a whole book on this subject alone. Therefore we will go over enough basic detail as we can to get you on your way to getting yourself a great deal.

During your initial contact and meet and greet stages you have been setting the stage for this moment and now it is time to get to the nitty gritty and talk numbers. Both buyers and sellers have their role to play that will help themselves get the best deals. Let's break it down for both sides and get you closer to getting a great deal.

Negotiating a deal for Buyers

When you were talking to the seller on the phone you may have asked them already what their best price is. Know that most sellers have a price in their head that is their bottom line and that when they give you the price on the phone, they usually still leave some wiggle room above their bottom line (especially if they have read this book!).

On the phone you can also ask what the best price they could give you is if you were to come right away with cash. This is your first offer attempt and if they don't budge yet don't worry too much. Do not "lowball" or make an offer on the phone that is extremely low and insulting to the seller. This could not only hurt your chances of negotiating a good deal later but could also keep the seller from allowing you to even look at the item. Be fair and reasonable as there is usually room for negotiations in person.

Once a price is agreed upon on the phone you are ready to go look at the item and try to get an even better deal. You will now be assessing the item based on what you see. On the phone you were making an offer "sight unseen" and the seller knows this as well. Negotiating more in person is much easier as you are standing there ready to take the item and they know you have the cash and are a serious buyer.

There is usually more to the story about the item once you get to see it in person including flaws the seller may have either forgotten to mention or was failing to mention on purpose hoping no one would notice. This is why you need to do your research ahead of time and know what you are looking for.

When you are talking about the item with the seller, mentioning the pros and cons we went over in the last chapter, you are setting up for this negotiation stage. You are letting the seller know you are informed and that you know about and notice all about the item.

In some instances you will have to stick to the price that was agreed to on the phone, which is why we say to make sure you have the full amount on you when you go to meet with the seller. This is due to many factors and we will try to cover the most common ones in this chapter, but keep in mind there are more than we can cover in this book.

Some immediate factors can happen before you even get to view the item in the background. The seller may have already priced the item low in order to move it quickly and they don't have much wiggle room on the price if any.

There could also be a demand for the item at the price it has been listed at that could cause a surge in the amount of people contacting the seller. This could cause the seller to decide to either take their full asking price only, or even more than their asking price. How this may happen is if some people who really want the item start what's called a "bidding war" offering more money to the seller than they were asking in order to secure the item for themselves.

Sometimes the seller's personality or reasons behind them selling their item can be a large factor in negotiations as well. We will go through the different types of buyers and sellers in detail later in this book.

Sometimes the deal is already the best it can be therefore there is no need for negotiations as it could jeopardize whether you get the item or not. Sometimes it is just a quick grab and go situation or you may lose out.

For the cases where it seems like there is room for negotiations you will need to review the flaws you had pointed out to the seller and let them know that due to those issues you can give them "said dollar amount" right now and can then take away the item. You have now officially opened the negotiations.

The seller will most likely come back somewhat lower than your originally agreed on price from your phone conversation. Now you can throw numbers back and forth until you come to a final agreement which will usually be meeting somewhere in the middle.

Here is an example of what we were just talking about.

Example:

The items price in the ad was $1000. On the phone you asked what their lowest price on their item would be and they tell you $900. You agree to meet and bring the full $900 with you. After assessing the item further you remind the seller of the flaws you have found and offer the seller $600 due to the condition you now see the item in. The seller comes back at $800. You will now ask the seller to split the difference and meet you in the middle at $700. Most sellers will. This is one of the best and easiest ways that a negotiation can work.

But this is just an example of the way a smooth negotiation can go, but this is not always the case. As we said before there are many factors that can come into play when negotiating a deal.

Sometimes the seller may have more than one similar item for sale and this can not only help in your negotiations, but can get you an even potentially better deal. If you are interested in getting an even better deal then you must be willing to put out more money to do it. You will need to assess all of the items as you would do with just the item you originally went to see. Just as you would before, find out what the lowest price is but on all items. Then ask them what they would take for all the items combined in a packaged deal. The next step is to negotiate the packaged deal price like you would above, the more money you are handing the seller, the better deal you will usually get per item.

This process will usually bring down the price per item on all and give you an even better deal than you would have gotten on each item by itself. You may have had to put more money out but you have been successful at getting a great deal.

Due to the many differing factors that can erupt in the buying process you may not always be successful in securing yourself an amazing deal all the time, but the better you get at all of the processes in this book the better you will become as a buyer. You may start to find you come out on top more and more often.

Negotiations for the seller

As a seller it is good to know the tactics that your buyer may be using so we hope you have read the above section as well as yours. The points are great for you as well as the information to come.

You need to know that the art of negotiation starts during the initial contact phase not just when you meet with the buyer. Most times you will find a serious buyer will ask you what the lowest you will go is sight unseen. Never give your actual lowest price as you must leave room for further negotiations later. You can always go down in price later but not up.

While on the phone and especially in person do not let the buyer push you to a lower price than your rock bottom price. If the amount seems unreasonable to you, do not forget that you are in control and that there are always other buyers out there that may give you what you desire for your item, if you have it priced fairly. Trust in the price you have set for yourself and make sure you do not become your own enemy in this process by allowing the buyer to walk all over you.

If you have done all of the research then you should have your price set according to what it is worth. Don't give away your item for less than you are comfortable with…period. You are an honest seller hiding nothing with your item, if you are following this book, so be confident in your bottom line price and stick to it. You are in the driver's seat, don't let anyone try to take the controls from you!

Don't just stop here as the learning process is still not over. Read on for more important information, including insights into the art of trading and the different personalities you may encounter as a buyer or seller.

Chapter Six

Trading: Toasters, skateboards and guns...

oh my!

The information in this section will not be split for both buyers and sellers as the same information is beneficial to both in the same context. Getting a great deal doesn't always have to involve cash or at least not as much of it. You can make great deals using items you have that you would like to part with.

There are many ways trading can work in your favor depending on your motivation behind the item you want and what you have to trade. You can use items you have to trade in several different ways depending on their worth, condition and whether the item is desirable to the seller.

There are also several forms of trading that you will need to know that can help you acquire or work your way up to an item you desire. There are also many different ways you not only can use an item within a trading situation, but several different ways you can use a trade to benefit yourself.

But before we get too far, you need to do the research like you would a seller to have a definite value of your item, or items, you would like to trade in your mind. And you will need to ask during the initial contact with the seller if the seller would be interested in a trade of any kind. They will either say "no" or "what have you got?" If they are interested in finding out what you have to trade then you have one foot in the door.

Now we will cover what to trade to save yourself some cash. We have been offered some crazy things in the past, hence this chapters title. We have been offered toasters, game systems, knee boards, musical instruments, skate boards, and yes…guns.

It wasn't just that we had no want and need for the above items, the biggest problems were their value and resale in comparison to the item we were selling. If I am selling a $1500 quad, why would you offer me a used game system in which the price new doesn't even come close to what I am asking, let alone it's now used value? And as a straight across trade? I don't think so!

So that is why we want to cover the topic of what to offer and how first. You need to think that the person may want to sell your item to get money towards the one they sold you; therefore you need to be fair in your offer. Also you need to assess what the item is and its current value in comparison to what you're buying.

For Example: An older person selling their grown kids old dirt bike they had rode as a kid is most likely not interested in your game systems and skate boards for instance. It's a bad example but it is an example of how some who offer trades don't think things through before offering them for a trade.

It's best to stick to similar items of around the same category. It could be you would like a quad and have a dirt bike you're not using, see if the seller would be interested in a dirt bike. Vehicles are also great trades as most people will take a vehicle on trade whether they plan to use it or not, as it's a relatively easy sell. And you are not limited to just trading one item, you can trade several if the other person agrees, it's all in the value of the items.

The resale value on your item will help determine how you will trade as well. Remember, when trading you must do your research on your item as if you were to sell it yourself as to have a proper value in mind. Like selling, it doesn't matter as much what you paid for the item, it's what the next person can sell it for, the current value. Trading helps you get rid of an item you don't need to bring down the cost of an item you want.

There are 3 different types of trading depending on the value of your item you are offering to trade and the value of the item you are looking to trade for. These are the "dollar for dollar" trading types. You may offer a partial trade plus you provide some cash difference, a straight across trade, or if your item is worth more than their item, the seller gives you cash difference. The latter is the hardest to do and takes confidence and boldness.

There are also 3 ways that you can trade depending on your motivation for the item you want. You won't always be in a "dollar for dollar" scenario, like above, but these 3 ways you can trade can be tricky.

The first type you can do is what's called "trading down". This means that your item is worth more than the item you are trying to get, but you really want their item, and you just don't have the money to buy it, you can offer the trade straight across to motivate the seller to trade with you. Most people will have no problem trading you something of lesser value with something they can sell for more money.

The second type you can do is the one we mentioned above which is the "dollar for dollar straight across trade" which means the items are close to the same value, which we covered the different ways this can work above.

Then there's the third type, which is called "trading up". This one is the opposite of trading down as you come out with an item of more value in the end. Even though this is harder to do than trading down, it is not rare. Sometimes people would just rather have your item than the one they are selling and will trade you, especially if it's of no use to them and they don't need the cash for their item.

Trading is not as hard as it seems, but it is a skill in itself. You can offer trades from both a buyer and seller aspect, not just as a buyer. If you are selling an item because you need or want a different item, take a look through other seller's ads and consider offering them a trade like some of the ones we mentioned above. This can save you the time and effort of trying to sell your item.

Regardless of what type of trading you decide to do you still must go through all the steps in this book to get there, just like purchasing the item for cash. The difference is that you must also research your own item so that you not only have a value in mind, but that you can answer their questions about your item as well.

Just like the art of buying and selling, you can win and lose in trading so be diligent in all the steps in this book to protect yourself.

In the next chapter we will be going through the different types of buyers and sellers to watch for, and how to spot them.

Chapter Seven

All Types: The good, bad and ugly

What we will cover in this chapter is the most common types of buyers and sellers you will encounter in the buying and selling world. We will also try to give you what information we can on how to spot these people ahead of time, which can help you to avoid the ones you should steer clear of. Not all are necessarily bad; it can just be challenging to deal with them.

We will be breaking it down into 3 categories, the sellers, buyers and some that are part of both categories. We have not put them in any particular order, as they can strike in any order.

Let's get started...

Types of Sellers:

The "Doesn't care to sell" seller. This person will be stubborn and hard headed on their price. They won't move a penny on their price and they don't care if no one will buy it. With these sellers you will need to make sure the price is right for what it is and that you are okay with paying the amount they are asking. These people are easy to spot since they will tell you flat out they aren't going to sell the item for less. They also usually will put FIRM after their price in their ad and may even state "not a penny less" in their ad.

The "Desperate" seller. This person is the easiest to negotiate with. They usually need the money badly and will take almost anything for their item. You can tell these sellers by their ad wording. It may say things like "need gone ASAP", "cash only, need the money", "Must sell by *said day*", "priced to sell fast", and "best offer takes the item". Although the negotiations are easier with this type of seller, they usually still have a bottom line depending how much money they need.

The "Want it gone" seller. Although similar to the above seller, they aren't as hard up and won't just give their item away either. They still have a bottom line and won't budge off that. But they are easier to negotiate with. They use similar wording as the above in their ads such as "need gone ASAP", "moving, must sell", "priced to sell fast", and "best offer takes the item".

The "On the fence" seller. This seller can be very frustrating for buyers. This person doesn't know if they really want to sell their item and therefore they tend to drag their feet when it comes to meeting up and will hum and ha when you ask them their bottom line price. They sometimes dodge potential buyer's attempts to get in touch with them to buy their item. They may even go as far as deciding not to sell their item when you are physically at their location looking at it (yes, we have had this happen!). This is why one of the first things we cover for sellers in this book is to make sure without a doubt that you are ready and willing to sell your item. If not, you may become one of these sellers later on. This type of seller may also go as far as calling you after you bought the item wanting to buy it back. If someone seems unsure on when they want to meet and how much they want for their item STEER CLEAR as they may be this type of seller.

The "Fisherman" seller. This seller likes to post their item for sale with no price to see what people offer them. They like to start bidding wars and will not commit to any meetings or prices when contacted by a buyer. They may ask that you call back in a week, or say they won't be home for a while to buy themselves time to see what kind of offers come their way. Sometimes they have no intention of selling their item unless they get offers above what the value is, and even then they may still just keep it. Some ways to tell this type of seller is if they say things like "make an offer" or "email an offer" in their ad. They will also be hard to get a hold of and tend to put off reasonable offers and meetings to view the item for long periods of time. They may also tell you what the highest offer is so far on the item and tell you outright that they are taking offers right now.

The "Cutthroat" seller. This seller doesn't care who buys the item, just the bottom line. They will screw you over in a heartbeat for more money. This type of seller will tell you that if you get to their house before someone that is currently on their way you can have the item. They will even call you while you are on your way to meet them and tell you it's sold because they either had a better offer and/or they sold it out from underneath you because someone else showed up first. One of the ways to tell this type of seller is if they tell you something like "if you get here before the next guy that's on his way it's yours." Also if you offer them more money than a buyer that's on their way they will usually tell you they will cancel the other person, and you can come get it. This seller may also change the price before you meet them and tell you it is more money because they got a better offer. And sometimes all of this is actually lies, there never was another offer or person on their way so STEER CLEAR!

Types of Buyers:

The "Nothing better to do" buyer. I actually hate to even call them a buyer because they never actually buy anything, but love to waste your time acting like it. They may only go as far as asking one simple question "do you still have it?" or they may actually make you believe they want the item and ask you all sorts of questions about it. We also like to call them "picture collectors" as they will ask you to send them pictures or more pictures of your item and then you never hear from them again. These are time wasters and usually are too lazy to call, so they email and text instead.

The "Lowballer" buyer. This type of buyer is also only loosely termed as a buyer. The only time they might buy is if you are willing to nearly sell your item for nothing. They will give you an insanely low offer on your item, then act insulted that you deny their insultingly low offer. Since we have never actually said yes to one of their low offers we are not sure if they will actually show up to buy the item…probably not. Most of these people will only send their lowball offers through email and text like the above buyer type.

The "tire-kicker" buyer. This type of buyer is probably the most well-known and hated in the buying world. They are the ultimate time wasters. They will carry the entire process through like a serious buyer, then walk away at the end using excuses like "I have to think about it", "I have others to look at" or "I don't have the money yet to buy right now". They will even try to ask you to hold the item for a long period of time because they "for sure want to buy it". These people have nothing but time to waste so they will waste yours, and they feel no remorse about it. And like the above type, they like to lowball with no intention to buy.

Types that fall under both Buyers and Sellers:

The "Back peddler" This person always backs out on deals, trades and buying or selling. They will make excuses at the last second for not showing up or they won't call at all and leave you hanging. They will start to make deals with you then change their mind when the deal closure nears. Some excuses they will use are all the same such as "someone was in a car accident and I am going to the hospital". That is if you are lucky enough to get an excuse.

The "Curber" These people are in the middle of the buying and selling world. They are in the game to make money and will step on any one they can to get it, in both the buying and selling aspect. They are out to make a quick dollar and usually buy items low and sell them high. They are also some of the biggest liars, so you must beware. They do very little to nothing to what they buy to improve its condition to warrant a higher dollar. They usually have multiple ads for both selling similar items and looking to buy more items. They want to make the maximum profit they can and will be some of the worst "lowballers" in the game. Money is all they care about and they have no worries about who they screw over in the process.

The "Collectors" These people like to buy items cheap and hoard everything they buy claiming its part of their collection. They will sell or trade most times, but for far more than the item is worth because they think it's worth more (because it's a "collector's item" as far as they are concerned). They see everything as being a part of their collection, and that they need high dollars to part with it.

The "Freebee" These people like to pick up items for free and flip it to make good money. These people are similar to curbers but instead of buying items cheap they use sob stories in their ads to get items for free, yet they are quite picky on the free items they want or are willing to take. They may use stories like "looking for a project for me and my son to work on together, must be new as possible, run and drive…" etc. They use these stories to manipulate people into giving them free items that they can sell and make 100% profit.

The "Scammer" These people are honestly the scum of the buying and selling world. They make people lose their trust and make them more reluctant to buy. They will promise you the world in exchange for money upfront. They will tell you they have a buyer for your item for more money, just send them some money up front first. They will also try to scam buyers by advertising an item for way less money than the item is clearly worth (like for instance say a 2015 BMW car for $5000, yeah, totally legitimate right? WRONG!). Sometimes you may even see an ad for an item with something out of place in the pictures, like a foreign license plate, or palm trees in the background for an area that doesn't have palm trees. They have tainted everything from online websites to newspaper classified ads. They are usually easy to spot but still manage to pull the wool over some people's eyes. Unfortunately, there are way too many out there for the policing agencies to arrest them all, therefore the only advice I can give you is that if a deal seems too good to be true, its most likely is a scam. Also if anyone asks you to wire money through some sort of specific online site, it's probably a scam.

Although all of these types are not everyone who buys and sells these people are the most common that you may meet in the buying and selling world.

Final Thoughts

Now you have the tools you need to start getting yourself the great deals as well!

It may take time and practice, and reviewing sections of this book more than once, but you should find it getting easier, and that you are getting better and better deals as time goes on.

The information in this book is the basics of what you need to know and you can learn to customize these principals over time for yourself.

I didn't learn these skills overnight and it took trial, error and about 10 years of learning and development to get where I am today.

Luckily you get to have this book to help you with all the skills I have developed.

That is the purpose of all the information you just read through, you now have the short notes version to 10 years of trial and error.

Now you can take this information and put it into action.

I wish you all the best, GOOD LUCK!

About the Author

This book was a team effort and therefore we will cover information on both parties to this collaborative effort.

Bryan provided all the information in order for this book to exist. He has spent the last 10 years of his life developing the skills and information that has been shared in this book, and then some.

Bryan started working on cars and small engines as a kid, being taught some skills by his dad and the rest on his own. He used to take apart items then put them back together just to learn how they work.

He always had a passion for mechanics and making things run that didn't. It is still to this day a thrill to him to bring an item home and figure out what's wrong with it, then get it running.

You could almost say he is the "machine whisperer".

Roxanne also believed the information would make a great "how to" book and decided to sit down with Bryan and pick his brain for the information.

Roxanne has been a reader and lover of books since very little and has also been an avid writer since childhood.

She has had a passion to be an author of books since her teens and is currently working on a 5 book fiction series of her own.

She decided to take some time from her own works to write this book and release it first, as the information can be immediately helpful to so many people.

Together Bryan and Roxanne outlined all the information he had provided and formed the flow of this book from start to finish.

With all the information organized Roxanne set to writing, having Bryan go through each page and chapter as it was finished, to make sure the information was provided correctly and in an easy to read format.

Bryan has met so many people throughout the years that have asked him repeatedly "how do you do what you do?", and he decided it was time to get this information out there to teach others.

Bryan Desjardins   Roxanne Petersik

Share your thoughts

If you found the information in this book helpful in your life and would like to pass this book to your friends and family, we invite you to share this book on social media pages!

Please visit/like/ share and follow us:

Like our page on Facebook at www.facebook.com/roxannepetersikauthor

Send us a tweet and follow us on Twitter at @RoxannePetersik or twitter.com/RoxannePetersik

Follow us on Google+ at google.com/+RoxannePetersikAuthor

Subscribe to us on YouTube at youtube.com/c/RoxannePetersikAuthor

Send us an email to join our list for news, upcoming books and release dates at roxannepetersik@gmail.com

We also invite you to review this book

Buy/Sell/Trade: What You Need To Know! on Amazon

as feedback is always appreciated and

we would love to know which part of this book was most helpful to you!

Thank you very much!

CPSIA information can be obtained
at www.ICGtesting.com
Printed in the USA
BVHW051226230223
659071BV00016B/862